PYTHON PROGRAMMING

FOR BEGINNERS

Enter the Real World of Python and Learn How to Think

Like a Programmer

Table of Contents

INTRODUCTION

CHAPTER 1: INTRODUCTION TO PYTHON

CHAPTER 2: INSTALLING PYTHON

CHAPTER 3: IDLE AND PYTHON SHELL

CHAPTER 4: VARIABLES, EXPRESSION, AND STATEMENTS

CHAPTER 5: FUNCTIONS

CHAPTER 6: STRINGS METHOD

CHAPTER 7: CONDITIONAL STATEMENTS AND LOOPS

CHAPTER 8: LISTS

CHAPTER 9: DICTIONARY

CHAPTER 10: TUPLES

CHAPTER 11: CLASSES

CONCLUSION

Introduction

This book is for aspiring individuals who want to learn programming and those who wish to discover the world of Python. It's a guide that provides the language basics simply and clearly, trying to make you autonomous in programming.

The topics will let you familiarize you with how programs work and their primary components.

You will also find interesting examples and tasks that will make you start thinking about programming in a Python-oriented way.

The book will teach you the basics of Python programming concepts, starting from the simplest to the most complex. Here you'll encounter a sufficient number of examples and exercises to help you practice all these concepts. You can use these exercises as guidelines or take advantage of them to input your programming.

These samples will help you build everything from simple programs to complex ones. These tasks will not take too much time, but they'll be useful for you.

The first part is an overview of Python. It talks about what it is, how it works, and its objectives. The following chapters are about executing programs, getting input from the user, outputting to the screen, processing the data, file handling, objects, and classes, mathematical functions.

The later parts deal with applications of Python in scientific computing. The material is intended for programmers who want to get more precise information about the language or apply its principles in an area of their profession.

This book can be read independently but will get you farther if you take advantage of the exercises presented throughout. This will help you grasp all the concepts and start with your projects. It will be of great use for anyone with little or no experience in programming. At the same time, it is a good tool for those who want to improve their knowledge of Python and apply its principles in practice. This book is written with simplicity and clarity in mind. It doesn't require prior programming knowledge since it will teach you the basics right from the start. The author considers that people who read it may come from different backgrounds (geography, disciplines) or have previous experience in programming.

The book provides a good introduction to programming using Python as an example language. It consists of 11 chapters aimed at revising the most significant concepts related to this language. Each chapter focuses on a certain topic and is accompanied by examples, exercises, and applications in practice. The chapters are arranged to enable the reader to acquire the necessary knowledge to understand the framework of an application.

Python is used by many people, professionals, and amateurs alike. It is easy to learn, has powerful features, and provides all you need to create new programs or improve existing ones.

Chapter 1: Introduction to Python

What Is Python?

Python is a powerful, polyvalent programming language with a strong emphasis on readability. It offers code readability, extensibility, and data analysis capabilities that have attracted many users from academia and industry.

Python is used as a scripting language, but some benchmarks show it can be competitive as a systems programming language or even more efficient than others like C++ for some applications. Python's simplicity makes it popular with people who want to start in computer programming because it eases the difficulty of understanding basic concepts of programming languages. It is reasonably easy to make use of existing programmers written in Python. Content of Python is easy to learn and use. It is easy to use for many different purposes. Try writing some simple programs with Python on your computer or your cellphone. Try the new version of the apps that are made for android phones. They are usually written in Python, which means it's really easy to handle them with your phone if you know the command line on your phone.

The way that Python teaches new programmers seems simple, but it might be difficult at first because if you've never written a program before, it may seem incomprehensible what you need to do the first step by step. But when you get an idea of the language and how it works, you will always remember what you did and how to do the same things again. It's because Python has a lot of equality, and there are a lot of computer science terms in it, but they are all explained in a way that makes sense.

What Are the Origins of Python and Why

Python was developed by Guido Van Rossum between 1980 and 1991. He wrote its predecessor, a programming language called ABC when he was an undergraduate at the University of Nijmegen in the Netherlands. He extended ABC to add list objects and then renamed it to Python in honor of the British comedy group Monty Python. "I liked their irreverent approach to things," Van Rossum said in an interview with the website O'Reilly Media. "The whole team worked on a lot of different stuff and never stuck to one line."

Van Rossum released Python in January 1994, making it freely available for anyone to use or modify at no cost. After that, programmers began using it in their programs.

Python is an open-source language, meaning anyone can freely use or modify it. That has made it popular with both scientists and hobbyists. And because of the ease of learning, Python has made its way to computer science educational programs, XBOX games, web development and even found its way into the area of software engineering called software reliability engineering.

Python's success is evidenced by the number of people who have contributed to its development over the years. By 2006 there were nearly 3 million lines of Python code being used by developers worldwide daily.

The Name Python?

The name Python can easily refer to any snake or reptile that lives in the river. It is the name of a New York song by Harry Chapin and a long line of Unix tools. Van Rossum chose it as a tribute to Monty Python because "Python" sounds like an English word.

Van Rossum is not the only person who has used Python for naming software projects. Novell also uses python for its interoperability program, which allows people using different operating systems to use programs written in one language that will run on another system with little modification.

Software Quality

The open-source Python programming language has become the dominant scripting language for software development and scientific applications. The simplicity and speed of its syntax and core library make Python ideal for prototyping, scripting, and rapid application development across a wide range of application domains. Python has been used to create new applications such as wikis, email, chat servers, Google Earth plugins, browsers, games, and servers. Python's popularity is at an all-time high: it is used in multiple top 10 websites worldwide (e.g., Google, YouTube, and Twitter), it is the language of choice for scientific computing, it is the language of choice for educators, and it is being taught in schools across the world. Python has also been used to create a portable version of Tcl called Tkinter.

What Are the Benefits?

The benefits of Python include easy and interactive learning, readability, quick development, and prototyping. This language supports modular programming, information hiding, object-oriented programming, dynamic typing, and automatic memory management. There are no limits on the expressiveness or complexity of your code. Python can serve as a scripting language for web applications; it has also been used for commercial products, web services, and to create desktop applications.

What Are the Disadvantages?

The disadvantage of Python is the decision to use whitespace as formatting. To format your code with whitespace, you must use a text editor that supports this mode. This can be difficult to find, and it does not support word wrapping. In addition, it is difficult to find a complete set of libraries that can be used with Python. You can find a library for almost any programming application you need but it may not be a complete integrated solution.

To use Python effectively, you must understand the basic operation of the Python interpreter and the core object types and functions of the language. These objects include variables, comparison operators, control flow statements, input/output operations, and expressions. The various built-in data types include integers, floating-point numbers, strings, tuples, and lists, and dictionaries for storing objects in collections. In addition, directives such as import allow you to access other libraries for specific functions or modules that have been written with Python.

Who Used Python Today?

Python is being used by a lot of major players worldwide. For example, Google, YouTube, and Twitter have all been using the Python programming language to increase productivity. In addition to these great companies, python has also been used in many different schools worldwide. The popularity of the language is at an all-time high, with so many people using it for their desired goals. Since python is such a simple and concise language to work with, it makes it easier for people to learn, and they can also apply it to whatever they need for their purposes. Since the technology is easy to use, it can be used by students and business professionals for the different purposes that they may need and what python has been associated with. With so many people interested in this programming language, there will never be a shortage of those who want to learn more about what python has to offer.

Chapter 2: Installing Python

Python is a well-known programming language. Python may be considered an essential language as the English language. Python 2 and Python 3 are 2 significant renditions of Python. Be that as it may, Python Installation for both adaptations is unique. What's more, both the renditions' commands and way condition factors are unique. You can pick your Python form as indicated by your prerequisite. Fledglings consistently face difficulties in installing Python in their working framework. This chapter is for them. Here you will realize how to install Python in Windows, Linux, macOS. Also, you find here step-by-step instructions to check your Python renditions. Try to install Python cautiously by perusing every one of the means depicted here else it might be wrongly installed.

Python Installation for Windows

· Click on the "Downloads" icon from the official Python website and select Windows.

· Click on the "Download Python 3.8.0" button to view all the downloadable files.

· You will be taken to a different screen to select the Python version you would like to download. In this book, we will be using the Python 3 version under "Stable Releases." So scroll down the page and click on the "Download Windows x86-64 executable installer".

· A pop-up window titled "Python3.8.0-amd64.exe" will be displayed.

· Click on the "Save File" button to start downloading the file.

· Once the download has completed, double click the saved file icon, and a "Python 3.8.0 (64-bit) Setup" pop window will be displayed.

· Make sure that you select the "Install Launcher for all users (recommended)" and the "Add Python 3.8 to PATH" checkboxes. Note—If you already have an older version of Python installed on your system, the "Upgrade Now" button will appear instead of the "Install Now" button, and neither of the checkboxes will be displayed.

· Click on the "Install Now" button and a "User Account Control" pop-up window will be displayed.

· A notification stating, "Do you want to allow this app to make changed to your device" will be displayed. Click on Yes.

· A new pop-up window titled "Python 3.8.0 (64-bit) Setup" will be displayed, containing a setup progress bar.

· Once the installation has been completed, a "Set was successful" message will be displayed. Click on the "Close" button, and you are all set.

· Navigate to the directory where you installed Python to verify the installation and double click on the Python.exe file.

Python Installation for MacOS

MacOS is a working framework created by Apple Inc. It is much the same as the Windows Operating System and another working framework. The greater part of the more current adaptations of MacOS has pre-installed Python. You can check whether the Python is installed or not by the accompanying directions.

Download Python 3 or 2 new types. Python 3.6 or Python 2.7 was the fresher form at the hour of writing this. Download the Mac OS X 64-piece/32-piece installer. Run the bundle and follow the installation steps to install the Python bundles.

· Click on the "Downloads" icon from the official Python website and select Mac.

· Click on the "Download Python 3.8.0" button to view all the downloadable files.

· You will be taken to a different screen to select the Python version you would like to download. In this book, we will be using the Python 3 version under "Stable Releases." So scroll down the page and click on the "Download macOS 64-bit installer" link under Python 3.8.0, as shown in the picture below.

· A pop-up window titled "Python3.8.0-macosx10.9.pkg" will be displayed.

· Click on the "Save File" button to start downloading the file.

· Once the download has completed, double click the saved file icon, and an "Install Python" pop window will be displayed.

· Click on the "Continue" button to proceed, and a terms and conditions pop-up window will be displayed.

· Click "Agree" and then click on the "Install" button.

· A notification requesting administrator permission and password will be displayed. Simply enter your system password to begin the installation.

· Once the installation has been completed, an "Installation was successful" message will be displayed. Click on the "Close" button, and you are all set.

· Navigate to the directory where you installed Python to verify the installation and double click on the Python launcher icon to take you to the Python Terminal.

Linux

For Red Hat, CentOS, or Fedora, install the Python3 and Python3-devel packages.

For Debian or Ubuntu, install the Python3.x and Python3.x-dev packages.

For Gentoo, install the '=Python3.x*' ebuild (you may have to unmask it first).

· Click on the "Downloads" icon from the official Python website and select Linux/UNIX.

· Click on the "Download Python 3.8.0" button to view all the downloadable files.

· You will be taken to a different screen to select the Python version you would like to download. In this book, we will be using the Python 3 version under "Stable Releases." So scroll down the page and click on the "Download Gzipped source tarball" link under Python 3.8.0, as shown in the picture below.

· A pop-up window titled "Python3.7.5.tgz" will be displayed.

· Click on the "Save File" button to start downloading the file.

· Once the download has completed, double click the saved file icon, and an "Install Python" pop window will be displayed.

· Follow the prompts on the screen to complete the installation process.

Chapter 3: IDLE and Python Shell

There are 2 ways to run a Python program: using its runtime environment or the command line interpreter. The command-line interpreter has 2 forms. The first one is the regular Python shell. The second one is IDLE or Integrated Development and Learning Environment.

The regular Python shell uses the familiar command-line interface (CLI) or terminal look, while IDLE is a Python program encased in a regular graphical user interface (GUI) window. IDLE is full of an easy access menu, customization options, and GUI functions. At the same time, the Python shell is devoid of those and only offers a command prompt (i.e., the input field in a text-based user interface screen).

One of the beneficial functions of IDLE is its syntax highlighting. The syntax highlighting function makes it easier for programmers or scripters to identify between keywords, operators, variables, and numeric literals.

Also, you can customize the highlight color and the font properties displayed on IDLE. You only get a monospaced font, white font color, and black background with the shell.

All of the examples in this book are written in the Python shell. However, it is okay for you to write using IDLE. It is suited for beginners since they do not need to worry about indentation and code management. Not to mention that the syntax highlighting is truly beneficial.

Using an IDE

An IDE, which stands for Integrated Development Environment, is a program designed with several features that are useful to programmers.

It has a graphical interface, making typing code much faster due to autocomplete and history functions.

Programming stays the same whether you are using a text editor or an IDE; however, with the IDE, you will benefit from many shortcuts, reminders, and error signaling, and code autocorrect.

Many IDE's even include suggestions on how to fix an error.

There are many IDE's to choose from, but one of the most popular ones is IDLE.

It comes in the same package as Python, so there's no need to perform extra steps.

Remember that it can run in 2 modes, namely interactive and script.

Use interactive if you want Python to respond immediately to whatever commands you type.

Your First Program

Now that your toolkit is prepared, it's time to write your first program.

For this example, we'll use IDLE because it's important to get used to IDE's from the start to avoid any future frustrations.

If you prefer to use a text editor or the online Python console, go ahead, the code will work the same.

Now, start running IDLE in interactive mode.

You will now see a window that is known as a Python shell.

At the command prompt type the following line:

```
print ("Hello World!")
```

Now, you should see the result displayed on your screen like: Hello World!

That's it!

Congratulations, you can call yourself a programmer now.

Now let's discuss this bit of code briefly.

The first thing you'll notice is that Python code is plain English, easy to read and understand.

Even without programming knowledge, you probably knew what this line of code would do because it's self-explanatory.

That's the beauty of working with Python.

As for the command we used, "print ()" is a function that displays the text, which is written in the parentheses.

Remember that the line needs to be surrounded by quotation marks; otherwise, you'll get an error.

Furthermore, pay attention to how you type the function because everything is case-sensitive in Python.

The command "print" will work. However, if you type it as "Print," it will not.

Now, let's create the same program by using IDLE's script mode.

Don't forget that interactive mode gives you instant results.

It works the same as the online Python shell.

However, you won't be able to save your program so that you can continue working on it later.

You need to work in script mode to save and edit it later.

You can run IDLE in script mode simply by clicking on "File" and selecting "New Window".

Now type the same line again:

print ("Hello World!)

Hit the Enter key.

You'll notice that nothing happens.

That's because you are writing a list of instructions that will be executed later when you run the program.

First, you need to save the application by clicking on "Save As" from the "File" menu.

You'll notice that the file has the "py" extension by default.

Always make sure your scripts are saved this way to be recognized as Python programs.

If you run the program, IDLE will open the interactive mode window and display the result.

For now, you've run your "Hello World" program by using IDLE.

However, you normally want your applications to run like those you are currently using.

This means you want an executable file that you double-click and run.

At the moment, if you click on the Python file, a window will open and then close abruptly.

You may be thinking that the program doesn't work because nothing happened; however, something did happen.

It was simply too fast for you to observe anything concrete.

The program executed all of its instructions, which means that it displayed the message in a fraction of a second, and then it terminated itself.

You need to keep the program running once it executes all of its commands so that you can see the results and interact with them.

But before you do that, let's take a moment to discuss how to comment on your code and make it readable and easy to understand.

Chapter 4: Variables, Expression, and Statements

Assignment Statement

An assignment statement assigns a value to a variable or an item of data.

An assignment statement assigns values to variables, items of data, or whole lists. The basic format is:

<variable> = <expression>

The expression in the parentheses must evaluate to one of the following:

· A sequence or iterable that produces the desired number of items. This list may have both elements and sub-lists.

· One element will be replicated as many times as necessary to produce the desired number of items.

· An empty sequence, producing zero items. For example, consider this expression: "a = 3". It would assign 3 to "a."

Assignments in Python use "truthy" and "falsy" conventions to distinguish between values and those without. An assignment operation that would have no effect is considered "empty", so variables without a value are assumed to be empty unless specifically set to another object. In the following example:

· i = 0 is not an empty variable because it could be set to any type of value (including the value 0). On the other hand, an expression like codice_1 rarely has any effect other than assigning its argument to i. It is considered empty if the expression evaluates to anything other than codice_2. The Python interpreter makes this distinction when evaluating expressions as it parses statements.

Assignment statements with multiple targets can be chained together as follows:

· In this statement, first, the right-hand side of each assignment is executed, from right to left. Then the assignments of codice_3 and codice_4 are executed from left to right. If the statement were a single line, the first assignment would have been made before any other part.

· There must be no space between a keyword and its assignment target on the same line; otherwise, Python will interpret them as 2 separate statements.

Operators and Operands

An operand is a part of an expression that is either input into or output from a calculation. They are the other side to the equation that we see in our mathematical equations. An operator tells what action to take with those operands and what can be done with those results after it has been calculated.

Here are the operators for calculating:

Addition: +, *, /

Subtraction: -, * , /

Multiplication: x , * , ** . Divisibility by 7 : not divisible by 35 or 3 each time a number was multiplied by 7 it will be removed from the equation and replaced by 0 .

Division: /, x , //

Increment: ++, +

Decrement: --, -

Modulus (Remainder): %

Floor Division (remainder after division by 2): //

The following are operators for comparing numbers to each other or operators of equality and inequality. They are used for mathematical functions. < > = <> != != (not equal to) <= > >= (greater than or equal to) < (less than) <= ! ! (not equal to) == == (equal to) === === (equal to).

a == b == True if a and b are equal to each other. We do not talk about the equality of the operands, that is left to the comparison operator.

b != c will tell if a and b are not equal to each other, where both of them are numbers. All of the following (excluding None) return the value False , except None .

None! is Python's None . Python has nothing for which you can use None as an operator because it is not defined as an object - it doesn't exist. However, you can use None as an operand in some builtins like os .

a <= b is a shorthand notation for a <=> b where a and b are equal to each other.

a == None , is Python's None . When you encounter None as an operand, Python evaluates it as False .

You can also use the not operator on the left side of the comparison operator: o = not o

The following are operators for comparing objects.

x == y is True if x and y are equal to each other. If they are unequal, then False is returned. All of the following (excluding None) return the value False , except None .

None! is Python's None . Python has nothing for which you can use None as an operator because it is not defined as an object - it doesn't exist. However, you can use None as an operand in some builtins like os .

Expression and Statements

Beginners often ask many questions regarding how Python works. One of the major stumbling blocks that beginners face upon learning Python is their lack of understanding of the basic vocabulary for making the script works correctly.

Here are some expressions and statements in their simplest form to make this process easier. Briefly describe what each expression or statement means.

Expression: The "expression" represents a true or false value based on the execution of an instruction (in this case if).

Statement: The "statement" specifies what math operation should be performed on 2 input values and returns a single value as output.

· *if* statement: if statement in Python is used to evaluate the content of the conditional expression. The conditional expression, in this case, is "what if value1 > value2".

   o if the condition is True: It means that the code in the statement will be executed in case the condition is true.

   o if the condition is False: It means that the code in the statement won't be executed (in this case, you can skip this part)

· *else*: It means that none of the statements will be executed (in this case you can skip this part too).

· *print()*: This is used to print a string of characters to the screen. It can also be referred to as a "print statement."

· *else* statement: If an else statement is present, the remaining statements are skipped (you can skip this part too).

· *elif* statement: It means "else if" (in this case, if the function only needs one input, you will need another if)

· *while* loop: While loop in Python is used to execute a block of statements repeatedly until some condition evaluating false occurs.

· *for* loop: It is used to read several elements from a sequence or iterable object and iterate over them.

· The break statement: Used to stop the execution from completing the current code block.

· The continue statement

First Example

To create a simple script, open a new text file in notepad and write the following Python code:

```python
print("Hello! Welcome to Python")

print("Welcome to your first script")
while True:
print("Please wait. Loading...")
time.sleep(5)
continue # To skip the rest of the program
    print("Program continues here")
```

_____

```python
print("Bye, bye")
```

If you run this program, it would produce following result:

Hello! Welcome to Python Welcome to your first script Please wait. Loading... Program continues here _____ Bye, bye

Second Example

Write the following code into any file with the name 'sample2.py':

```python
print("This is the second example. Welcome to your second script")

print("Here, we are going to learn about the if condition")

number = int(input("Please enter a number: "))

if number > 10: # If the user enters a number greater than 10

print("The number is greater than 10")
```

else: # If they enter any other value

print("The number is less than or equal to 10")

Script Mode

Python programming can be used in several possible settings, from simple scripts to complete objectives. This will focus on the script mode, which is fast and easy to use.

#!/usr/bin/Python3

print("Hello, World!")

This script will print out "Hello World" when it is run—a classic introductory coding task. The first 2 lines tell the computer what language to use and where it's located on the operating system's path. The third line prints out our message to the user as a string without needing any variables or string manipulation functions.

The next section of the script is an if statement, which decides whether the user has entered a valid command or not. The final block of code will execute if the user enters "jays". If space is not the only character that the user enters, it will execute after multiple spaces.

An example of a script where Python would be used extensively is to build an IRC bot. A simple IRC bot can be used to automate many IRC tasks—for example, logging onto a server and downloading files without using an external program.

Order of Operations

One of the most important topics in programming is that of the order of operations. Almost all programmers follow 3 basic rules: Parentheses, Exponents, and Multiplication and Division. These 3 rules are called the standard order of operations rule. However, other orders can be followed depending on what you're doing with your code at any given time. One such difference is where you put functions inside your code; functions act as variables that must be ordered before all mathematical operations (functions cannot be manipulated with math).

Parentheses ()

Parentheses have the highest order of operations. Any time you surround a mathematical operation with parentheses, you tell Python to do all calculations inside the parentheses before continuing. For instance:

>>> (7+3)*11/2 >>> (7 + 3) * 11 / 2 >>> (7 + 3) * 11 / 2 50

We do not write the parentheses in each expression in the above code. Instead, we tell Python to calculate all of the expressions inside the parentheses before moving on. We can see this by looking at how Python calculates an expression.

>>> (7+3)*11/2 >>> 7+3 * 11/2 >>> 7 + 3 * 11/2 13.5

Python first calculates multiplication, then adds an exponent, and finally divides the product. First, Python calculates the multiplication of the 2 numbers, and then it multiplies the exponent by itself twice to raise it to a higher power. Next, Python divides each of the terms by 2.

(7+3)*11/2 = 13.5

The parentheses are the only operators that move to the top of the order of operations when used. You can use multiple levels of parentheses, however they are always calculated from inner-most to outer-most. Take a look at this example:

>>> (((7+3)*11)/2) + 2 >>> ((((7+3)*11) / 2) + 2) >>> (((7 + 3) * 11) / 2) + 2 >>> (((7 + 3) * 11) / 2) + 2 >>> (((7+3)*11)/2) +2

First, Python calculates all math inside parentheses. Then, Python calculates all math inside brackets around parenthesis. Finally, Python calculates all math outside of parenthesis and brackets.

Exponents (^)

The exponent rule determines that multiplication or division must be performed before exponents are converted to their corresponding base. For example:

>>> *3^2 >>> 3 * 2 >>> 4 >>> 8*

* (multiplication) / (division) \ (subtraction) + (addition/subtraction) <-> parenthesis

Hence, the order of operations is left-to-right, top-to-bottom. Parentheses are placed at the top, multiplication () and division () are placed at the bottom, addition () and subtraction () come next, negation () is last. Parentheses affect the order of evaluation, not the order that operations are done. First, Python evaluates the expression enclosed in parentheses. Then, it uses the expression inside parenthesis as long as needed. The expression outside of parenthesis is evaluated only once after calculating all expressions within. This means that an expression inside parentheses can be calculated before it is used to calculate another expression.

Multiplying exponents using the * operator will produce a wrong answer if you use 1/2 instead of 2/3. However, it will compute correctly when you compute the following:

1*2^3 = 1*2^9 = 2^9 = 32

And this:

1/2^3 = 1/2^(3-1) = 1/4= 1/12= 0.5

The reason for these results is that the * operator works on the exponent of the first operand, whereas ** works on the exponent of both operands.

>>> *1*2**3 = 1*2^(3+1) = 2^(3+1) = 32*

>>> *1/2**3 = 1/(2^(3-1))= 12/4=3/16=0.25*

The ** operator can also be used in combination with * for example: x^y, but because the ** operator works on the exponent of both operands, it has to use parenthesis around both operands before calculating their exponents. The result is different from the previous example because the numbers were multiplied, not exponentiated. The use of parenthesis prevents this behavior.

* and ** Both Operators: It is important to note that most programming languages do not support the exponentiation operator **. If this is your first programming experience, you may find that most languages do not provide any exponentiation operations. This is unfortunate, but it is not because of any technical limitation. Arithmetic in most programming languages has always been implemented in the "traditional" order (bottom to top.) Therefore, traditional arithmetic operations (including the ** operator) are performed for you by Python.

Modulus Operator

A common programming operator in Python is the modulus operator. This little character is represented by a percent sign and is used to perform modular arithmetic. What does that mean? It means that when you are using it in your code, it will return the remainder when one number is divided by another. For example, 9%4=1 because 4 goes into 9 with a remainder of 1 since 9 has no leftovers when divided by 4.

Why use the modulus operator? Modular arithmetic will help you do some math divisions more easily. It can be helpful if you try to do anything with numbers in your code, like dividing 2 numbers together but having no built-in function. Here is an example of how to use it.

1. Start with the number you want to divide with the modulus operator or find the remainder when that number is divided by another number.

2. Add the % character to the beginning of your original number, so you have something like this: %0=Result.

3. To subtract one value from another with this, subtract the value you are subtracting from what you are subtracting it from by using a - sign along with your modulus operator.

4. Put the modulus operator at the beginning of your original number, so you get something like this: %1-4=-2.

5. You can also use the modulus operator to compare or equal 2 numbers instead of just using equal signs and values and will get values like true and false.

6. Do NOT use quotation marks around your operands with modular arithmetic.

The modulus operator is not used often, but it does have useful applications for solving math problems with calculations. It can also be used with the bitwise operator, which allows you to solve problems with number encoding or data conversion.

String Operations

Python string operations are great because they are very flexible. One of the most useful operations is changing the case of a string. This is sometimes necessary to indicate that one string is used for upper-case or mixed-case text, while another has no capital letters. To change the case of a string, simply use xlower(), xupper(), or title() functions on it:

"Hello WORLD!" >>> "hello world!" 'HELLO WORLD!' >>> "HELLO WORLD!"

'Hello World!' >>> "Hello World!"

"HelloWorld." >>> "hello world." HELLOWORLD.

Helloworld." >>> "Hello World." HELLOWORLD.

'HelloWorld.' >>> 'HelloWorld.' HELLOWORLD.

'HELLO WORLD!' >>> 'HELLO WORLD!' HELLOWORLD.

>>> "Hello World." HELLOWORLD.

The title() function converts the title case into all lower-case letters without the first character (called "superscripts"). For example, if "This is a prepositional sentence", "this sentence", and "this is a sentence" are the same sentence, the following sentence would be This is a prepositional sentence:

The title() function can also convert to mixed-case or categories other than upper-case or all-lower-case. The first character of the first letter of each word is used as a "sign" to indicate what type of conversion is being made.

Asking the User for Input

The Python programming language is a powerful tool for doing computational work. The most basic of all interactions in Python is obtaining user input with the raw_input function. This tutorial will ask the user to enter their name and age.

In Python, a programming statement consists of a number of parts:

f = open('name') name = f.readline()

age = int(input('Enter your age: '))

f.close() print('Hello {}! You are {} years old.' .format(*name, *age))

We begin by opening the file named "name". If the file does not yet exist, it will be created. If the file already exists, we will overwrite its contents with the new data we write. Calling readline() on f reads a line from the file and stores it in name. We then ask the user to enter their age and convert their answer into an integer by calling int(input()).

Python provides a format statement to format outputs using dynamic values. The format statement is explained in more detail here: Formatting Output

Output:

The user's input will be automatically stored in name and age. Before printing our greeting, we use .format() to format the greeting. The *name, *age portion of the format statement represents the value of each variable.

f = open('name') # If name does not exist, create it; if it does, overwrite it.

name = f.readline() # Read a line from name and store it in name.

To obtain input from the user, use raw_input(). This stores input as a string in your script's memory until you request it be read into a variable. To convert a string into an integer or float, use int() or float(). The next example asks the user to enter their name and age and prints a greeting.

Input:

f = open('name') # If name does not exist, create it; if it does, overwrite it.

name = f.readline() # Read a line from name and store it in name.

age = int(input('Enter your age: ')) # Convert user's input into an integer if possible, otherwise return 0.

f.close() print('Hello {}! You are {} years old.'.format(*name, *age))

Output:

f = open('name') # If name does not exist, create it; if it does, overwrite it.

Open your file in write mode and write the data inside the variable name to the file. Close the file to save your changes. Note that we use f.write(name) instead of f.write(str(name)). The str() function converts a variable into its string representation (e.g., "Aidan" or 'Kate').

What Are Variables?

The computer stores the data that your program uses or will use in its RAM. The computer first finds a space in the RAM and allocates that space for the data your program needs. All the computer needs to do when the program and computer need the data is to find that space and retrieve it. The name is given to the specific location (within the RAM) where the data has stored the variable. So to say, a variable is a named location of data.

Note that the RAM is like a hotel that only offers transient lodging. The main difference is that the RAM has thousands and millions of rooms /addresses depending on its size. The computer searches for a vacant room or address when it needs to store data. The computer finds a room, gives the program's room number, and instructs the computer to store the data to that room number.

This process is a relatively easy task for the computer and your computer program. However, it can be problematic for you as a computer programmer. Why? Remember that the RAM is a huge hotel with thousands and millions of rooms, and data comes in and out of it every second your computer is on.

Say that you have text data that contains the word "Pedro." You want the program to store that information on the computer. The computer will then find space for it in the RAM.

The computer finds room 1,151,112 vacant and assigns/stores "Pedro" in it. When it is time for you to call or reference "Pedro," you need to tell the computer that you want the program to retrieve "Pedro" from rooms 1,151,112. It seems easy, right? Remember that in programming, memory addresses are often written using hexadecimal notation (i.e., a simple and expeditious way to encode binary numbers for modern computer systems in which a byte is defined as containing 8 binary digits). The room number 1,151,112 is written as 0x119088 in hexadecimal notation. This simple resource will show you how to convert a decimal to hexadecimal.

The first problem is that the RAM is a transient hotel. The data you will store will be in a different room number if 1,151,112 happen to be occupied when you start the program again. Memorizing the room number or address is already a difficult thing.

You might think that a good solution is instructing the computer to find the text "Pedro," right? It seems reasonable, but what if your text data contains all the text in a Harry Potter book? You cannot type all of those in your computer program repeatedly just to find them in your computer's RAM. Also, what if your data is an image? You cannot search for an image by using text.

The second problem is data duplicates. What if other programs have text data "Pedro" as well? Things can get messy quickly if you reference data from another program. What will happen to the other program that owns that data if you process and change that data?

The solution to the problems above is to make use of variables. Variables have 3 basic components: data, identifier, and address. You already know what data is. The identifier is a letter, word, or combination of letters, numbers, and symbols, which you can use to name the address of your data. On the other hand, the address is its location or address in your computer's RAM.

For example, you can tag it with a name instead of memorizing your data's room number/address. The computer assigned the text data "Pedro" to room 1,234,456. Instead of referencing that room number to find "Pedro," you can assign an identifier to it like text name (i.e., text name = Pedro).

The computer program creates a directory of sorts, which contains pointers to your data in the memory to make it easier for you and you to find the data in RAM. Here is a sample variable directory for a simple calculator program that is going to perform an addition operation to the numbers 12 and 436:

Identifier	Data	Memory Address
firstNumber	12	0xff456e
secondNumber	436	0x5e4775
operation	"+"	0x6f1106
result	448	0x1ca607

In older programming languages, you need to deal with memory addresses. The compiler will handle most memory-related concerns like storing and garbage collection (i.e., freeing up space in the RAM by removing unused/redundant data).

Aside from identifiers, data, and addresses, variables also have other data type and size components. Strongly typed programming languages like C and Java require programmers to declare the variable and the type of data it will contain. Stronger and stricter programming languages like Pascal require a declaration of the variable's size and type.

Python is also a strongly typed language, but it does not require programmers to declare variables and type. For example, creating a variable in Python is as simple as assigning a value or data to an identifier.

>>> x = 1

>>> _

With that simple statement, the program will create the variable x and assign a value of 1 to it. If you type the variable's identifiers in the command line, the interface will return its value.

>>> x

1

```
>>> _
```

Remember that if a variable does not exist in the program, Python or your program will return an error. For example:

> >>> *y*
>
> *Traceback (most recent call last):*
>
> *File "<stdin>", line 1, in <module>*
>
> *NameError: name 'y' is not defined*
>
> >>> _

The above error message might appear as gibberish for beginners. Fear not. Later in this book, I will show you how to read and handle errors.

Naming Variables

You must remember the following rules when creating and using an identifier or name for your variable:

· Your identifier must start with either an underscore or a letter.

· Your identifier must never start with a number. The program will return an error if this occurs. Your program and Python will consider any number you type after a space as a number. You cannot use a number as an identifier. Your numbers cannot contain letters or symbols except when writing in a different numeric notation (e.g., hexadecimal 0x12E4).

· Your identifier must only contain letters, numbers, and underscores.

· Your identifier is case-sensitive. This means that identifier X is different from identifier x.

· Your identifier can be as short as 1 character (e.g., x, _, y, etc.).

· Your identifier must not be the same as a keyword (these are reserved words, e.g., return, True, False, etc.) or a function.

Not following or adhering to these simple rules may lead to errors or unintended results in your program.

Assignment of Variable

Look at variables as a name linked to a specific object. In Python programming, you don't need to declare variables before using them like in other programming languages. Instead, you assign a value to a variable and begin to use it immediately. The assignment occurs using a single equals sign (=):

Y= 100

The same way a literal value can be shown from the interpreter using a REPL session, so it is to a variable:

· Later if you assign a new value to Y and use it again, the new value is replaced.

· Still, Python has room for chained assignments. In other words, you can assign the same value to different variables at the same time.

Example:

```
>>> a = b = c = 300
>>> print(a, b, c)
300 300 300
```

This chained assignment allocates 300 to the 3 variables simultaneously. Most variables in other programming languages are statically typed. This means that a variable is always declared to hold a given data type. Now any value assigned to this variable should be similar to the variable's data type.

However, variables in Python don't follow this pattern. A variable can hold a value featuring a different data type and later be re-assigned to hold another type.

Expressions

Expressions are lines of codes that perform operations using operators, which the program or computer evaluates to return a result. The term expression in programming is like Algebraic expressions wherein variables or data are placed on an operator's left and right sides. For example, 1 + 2 is an expression.

Expressions have multiple components: constants, variables, data, operators, delimiters, parentheses, functions, and results or output. In the expression 1 + 2, 1 and 2 are data, + is the operator, and 3 is the output.

There are multiple types of expressions. They are arithmetic, relational/comparison, Boolean/logical, string, bitwise, and mixed expressions. The type of expression you create depends on the operators you use and the data type of your expected result.

Your program is all about expressions. Expression mostly dictates the processing of data in your program. You can also use it in different scenarios. The most common scenario is to assign an expression's output to a variable.

Example 1:

```
>>> x = 1 + 2

>>> x

3

>>> _
```

Example 2:

```
>>> operandFirst = 1
```

>>> *operandSecond = 2*

>>> *output = operandFirst + operandSecond*

>>> *output*

3

>>> _

Operators

Python, just like with many programming languages, has numerous operators like arithmetic operators addition (+), subtraction (-), multiplication (*), and division (/). Some of those operators have similar functionalities in most programming languages.

Operators are divided according to their functionality and the data type of expression or output they produce. Most operators use signs and symbols, while some use keywords. Some operators use functions to perform uncommon or advanced data processing.

Note that not adding space between operands and operators will work. However, you should avoid typing expressions like that to prevent potential syntax errors.

Arithmetic Operators

Operation	Operator	Description	Example

Addition	+	Adds numbers	>>> 1 + 1
			2
			>>> _

Subtraction	-	Subtracts numbers	>>> 10 - 12
			-2
			>>> _

Multiplication	*	Multiplies numbers	>>> 42 * 35
			1470
			>>> _

Division	/	Divides the left-hand number by the right-hand number	>>> 132 / 11
			12
			>>> _

Floor Division	//	Divides the left-hand number by the right-hand number and returns only the whole number, effectively removing any decimal value from the quotient	>>> 10 // 3
			
			3
			
			>>> _

Modulus	%	Performs a floor division on the left-hand number by the right-hand number and returns the remainder	>>> 133 / 11
			1
			>>> _

Exponent	**	Raises the left-hand number by the right-hand power	>>> 4 ** 2
			16
			>>> _

Operation	Operator	Description	Example

Is Equal to	==	Returns true if left and right hand sides are equal	>>> 999 == 999
			True
			>>> _

Is Not Equal to	!=	Returns true if left and right hand sides are not equal	>>> 24 != 123
			True
			>>> _

Is Greater Than	>	Returns true if left-hand side's value is greater than the right-hand's side	>>> 554 > 64
			True
			>>> _

Is Less Than	<	Returns true if left-hand side's value is lesser than the right-hand's side	>>> 16 < 664
			True
			>>> _

Is Equal or Greater Than	>=	Returns true if left-hand side's value is greater or equal than the right-hand's side	>>> 554 >= 64
			True
			>>> 554 >= 554
			True
			>>> _

Is Equal or Less Than	<=	Returns true if left-hand side's value is lesser or equal than the right-hand's side	>>> 16 <= 664
			True
			>>> 16 <= 16
			True
			>>> _

Operation	Operator	Description	Example

Assign	=	Assigning the value of the right-hand operand to the variable on the left	>>> x = 1
			>>> x
			1
			>>> _

Add and Assign	+=	Adds the value of the left variable and the value of the right-hand operand and assign the result to the left variable	>>> x = 14
			>>> x
			14
			>>> x += 16
			>>> x
			30
			>>> _

Subtract and Assign	-=	Subtracts the value of the left variable and the value of the right-hand operand and assign the result to the left variable	>>> x = 30
			>>> x
			30
			>>> x -= 4
			>>> x
			26
			>>> _

Multiply and Assign	*=	Multiplies the value of the left variable and the value of the right-hand operand and assign the result to the left variable	>>> x = 26
			>>> x
			26
			>>> x *= 10
			>>> x
			260
			>>> _

Divide and Assign	/=	Dividing the value of the left variable by the value of the right-hand operand and assign the result to the left variable	>>> x = 260
			>>> x
			260
			>>> x /= 13
			>>> x
			20
			>>> _

Floor Divide and Assign	//=	Performs a floor division on the value of the left variable by the value of the right-hand operand and assign the quotient as a whole number to the left variable	>>> x = 20
			>>> x
			20
			>>> x //= 3
			>>> x
			6
			>>> _

Modulus and Assign	%=	Performs a floor division on the value of the left variable by the value of the right-hand operand and assign the remainder of the quotient to the left variable	>>> x = 6
			>>> x
			6
			>>> x %= 4
			>>> x
			2
			>>> _

Exponent/Raise and Assign	%=	Raises the value of the left variable by the power of the value of the right-hand operand and assigning the result to the left variable	>>> x = 2
			>>> x
			2
			>>> x **= 3
			>>> x
			8
			>>> _

Operation	Operator	Description	Example
Logical And	and	If both operands are true. Returns true	>>> True and True True >>> _
Logical Or	or	if one of the operands is true. Returns true	>>> True or False True >>> _
Logical Not	NOT	Returns the negated logical state of the operand	>>> not True False >>> _

If both operands are true, then the operator will only return true. It will always return False otherwise. The operator or will only return False if both operands are False. Otherwise, it will always return True. The operator will not return False if the operand is True and if the operand is False.

Below are truth tables for operator 'and' and 'or.'

Left Operand	Logical Operator	Right Operand	Result
True	And	True	True
True		False	False
False		True	False
False		False	False

Left Operand	Logical Operator	Right Operand	Result
True	or	True	True
True		False	True
False		True	True
False		False	False

Operation	Operator	Description	Example

In	In	Returns True if left operand's value is present in the value of the right operand	>>> x = "cat and dog"
			>>> a = "cat"
			>>> b = "dog"

			>>> c = "mouse"
			>>> a in x
			True
			>>> b in x
			True
			>>> c in x
			False
			>>> _

Not In	not in	Returns true if left operand's value is not present in the value of the right operand	>>> x = "cat and dog"
			>>> a = "cat"
			>>> b = "dog"
			>>> c = "mouse"
			>>> a not in x
			False
			>>> b not in x
			False
			>>> c not in x
			True
			>>> _

Operation	Operator	Description	Example

Is	is	Returns True if the left operand's identity is the same as the identity of the right operand
		Note: It may return True if the values of the operands are equal, but Python evaluates the identity or ID and not the values.
			>>> x = "a"
			>>> id(x)
			34232504
			>>> id("a")
			34232504
			>>> x is "a"
			True
			>>> x * 2
			'aa'
			>>> x * 2 is "aa"
			False
			>>> id(x * 2)
			39908384

Operation	Operator	Description	Example

		Equal values of a single data or variable tend to receive similar IDs. Results of expressions may receive new IDs or overlap with existing IDs with similar values. To check the ID of variables and data, you need to use the id() keyword/function. If you want to compare if values of the operands are equal, use == operator instead.	>>> id("aa")
			39908552
			>>> x * 2 is 2 * x
			False
			>>> id(x * 2)
			39908552
			>>> id(2 * x)
			39908384
			>>> _

Is Not	is not	Returns True if left operand's identity is not the same with the identity of the right operand	>>> x = "a"
			>>> id(x)
			34232504
			>>> id("a")
			34232504
			>>> x is not "a"
			False
			>>> x * 2
			'aa'
			>>> x * 2 is not "aa"
			True
			>>> _

.

Operation	Operator	Description	Example

Bitwise And (AND)	&	Returns 1 for bits if both operands have 1 on the same place value. Returns 0 for 0-0, 1-0, and 0-1 combinations.	>>> 0b1101 & 0b1001
			9
			>>> bin(9)
			'0b1001'
			>>> _

Bitwise Or (OR)	|	Returns 0 for bits if both operands have 0 on the same place value. Returns 1 for 1-1, 1-0, and 0-1 combinations.	>>> 0b1101 | 0b1001
			13
			>>> bin(13)
			'0b1101'
			>>> _

Bitwise Exclusive Or (XOR)	^	Returns 1 for bits if both operands have 0 and 1 on the same place value. Returns 0 for 1-1 and 0-0 combinations.	>>> 0b1101 ^ 0b1001
			4
			>>> bin(4)
			'0b100'
			>>> _

Bitwise Complement	~	Flips each bit and negates the value	>>> ~0b1010
			-11
			>>> bin(-11)
			'-0b1011
			>>> _

Bitwise Left Shift	<<	Moves bits of the left operand to left. The number of shifting of bits is according to the value of the right operand.	>>> 0b1010 << 2
			40
			>>> bin(40)
			'0b101000'
			>>> _

Bitwise Left Shift	>>	Moves bits of the left operand to right. The number of shifting of bits is according to the value of the right operand.	>>> 0b1010 >> 2
			2
			>>> bin(2)
			'0b10'
			>>> _

Left Operand	Logical Operator	Right Operand	Result
1	&	1	1
1		0	0
0		1	0
0		0	0

Left Operand	Logical Operator	Right Operand	Result
1	|	1	1
1		0	1
0		1	1
0		0	0

Left Operand	Logical Operator	Right Operand	Result
1	^	1	0
1		0	1
0		1	1
0		0	0

Create code for the following scenarios.

Create 5 separate expressions that will lead to a result of 10025. You cannot use an arithmetic operator more than once, and your first number must be 7.

Find the statistical mean of 10 survey respondents' ages. The ages are 18, 21, 19, 52, 6, 33, 15, 46, 72, and 25.

Find the value of x using these details:

x = y + (a * b / c)

y = a + 151

b = c * (144 + y)

y = 10

c = 7

Johnny was born on February 14, 1967. How many days old was he on January 1, 2000?

A car was moving 20 miles per hour on a straight road. Every five minutes, it instantly decelerates by 5 miles per hour and keeps that speed for a minute, and then instantly accelerates back to 20 miles per hour. How many miles will the car cover if it moves like that for an hour?

Chapter 5: Functions

When you are working with a language like Python, there will be times when you will need to work with something that is known as a function. These functions will be reusable code blocks that you will use to get your specific tasks done. But when you define one of these functions in Python, you need to have a good idea of the 2 main types of functions that can be used and how each of them works. The 2 types of functions available here are known as built-in and user-defined.

The built-in functions are the ones that will come automatically with some of the packages and libraries that are available in Python. Still, we will spend our time working with the user-defined functions because these are the ones that the developer will create and use for special codes they write. In Python, though, one thing to remember, no matter what kind of function you are working with, is that all of them will be treated like objects. This is good news because it can make working with these functions easier than we may see with some other coding languages.

The user-defined functions that we will talk about in the next section will be important and can expand out some of the work we are doing. But we also need to look at some of the work that we can do with our built-in functions. The list above includes many of the ones found inside the Python language. Take some time to study them and see what they can do to help us get things done.

Why Are User Defined Functions So Important?

To keep it simple, a developer will have the option of writing out some of their functions, known as a user-defined function, or they can go through and borrow a function from another library, one that may not be directly associated with Python. These functions will sometimes provide us with a few advantages depending on how and when we would like to use them in the code. Some of the things that we need to remember when working on these user-defined functions and gain a better understanding of how they work, will include:

· These functions are going to be made out of reusable code blocks. It is necessary only to write them out once, and then you can use them as many times as you need in the code. You can even take that user-defined function and use it in some of your other applications as well.

· These functions can also be very useful. You can use them to help with anything you want, from writing out specific logic in business to working on common utilities. You can also modify them based on your requirements to make the program work properly.

· The code will often be friendly for developers, easy to maintain, and well-organized all at once. This means that you can support the approach for modular design.

· You can write out these types of functions independently. And the tasks of your project can be distributed for rapid application development if needed.

· A user-defined function that is thoughtfully and well-defined can help ease the process for the development of an application.

Now that we know a little more about the basics of a user-defined function, it is time to look at some of the different arguments that can come with these functions. Then, we will move on to some of the codes you can use with this kind of function.

Options for Function Arguments

Any time you are ready to work with these kinds of functions in your code, you will find that they can work with 4 types of arguments. These arguments and the meanings behind them will be pre-defined, and the developer will not always be able to change them up. Instead, the developer will have the option to use them but follow the rules with them. You do get the option to add a bit to the rules to make the functions work the way that you want. As we said before, there are 4 argument types you can work with, and these include:

· **Default arguments:** In Python, we will find that there is a bit different way to represent the default values and the syntax for the arguments of your functions. These default values will be the part that indicates that the argument of the function is going to take that value if you don't have a value for the argument that can pass through the call of the function. The best way to figure out where the default value is will be to look for the equal sign.

· **Required argument:** The next type of argument will be the required argument. These are the kinds of arguments that will be mandatory to the function you are working on. These values need to go through and be passed in the right order and number when the function is called out, or the code won't run the right way.

· **Keyword arguments:** These are going to be the argument that will be able to help with the function call inside Python. These keywords will be the ones that we mention through the function call, along with some of the values that will go all through this one. These keywords will be mapped with the function argument so that you can identify all of the values, even if you don't keep the order the same when the code is called.

· **Variable arguments:** The last argument that we will take a look at here is the variable number of arguments. This is a good one to work with when you are not sure how many arguments will be necessary for the code you are writing to pass the function. Or you can use this to design your code where any number of arguments can be passed, as long as they have been able to pass any of the requirements in the code you set.

Writing a Function

Now that we have a little better idea of what these functions are like and some of the argument types available in Python, it is time for us to learn the steps you need to accomplish all of this. There are going to be 4 basic steps that we can use to make all of this happen, and it is really up to the programmer how difficult or simple you would like this to be. We will start with some of the basics, and then you can go through and make some adjustments as needed. Some of the steps that you need to take to write out your user-defined functions include:

· Declare your function. You will need to use the "def" keyword and then have the function's name come right after it.

· Write out the arguments. These need to be inside the 2 parentheses of the function. End this declaration with a colon to keep up with the proper writing protocol in this language.

· Add in the statements that the program is supposed to execute at this time.

· End the function. You can choose whether you would like to do it with a return statement or not.

An example of the syntax that you would use when you want to make one of your user-defined functions includes:

def userDefFunction (arg1, arg2, arg3, …):

program statement1

program statement2

program statement3

....

Return;

Working with functions can be a great way to ensure that your code will behave the way you would like. Making sure that you get it set up properly and that you can work through these functions, getting them set up in the manner that you would like, can be really important. There are many times when the functions will come out and serve some purpose, so taking the time now to learn how to use them can be very important to the success of your code.

Python functions are groups of related statements that perform a specified task. They help split the program down into more manageable chunks, useful if you are writing a large program. It also stops your code from becoming repetitive and allows you to reuse code. The syntax of a function looks like this: def function_name(parameters):

""""docstring""""

statement(s)

The definition of a function contains the following:

· The reserved keyword, def, starts the header of the function.

· The name of the function—function naming conventions are the same as for variables.

· The arguments or parameters that we pass the values through to the function—these are optional.

· A colon to end the header.

· Docstring—a documentation string to say what the function will do—this is optional.

· At least one statement, each one indented to 4 spaces.

· Return statement for returning the function value—this is optional.

The following example shows you a function:

def greet(name):

"""This function will greet

the person passed in as

parameter"""

print("Hello, " + name + ". Good morning!")

Function Call

Once the function has been defined, it can be called from another program, function or the command prompt and to do this, we type the name of the function and the parameters needed for it:

>>> greet('Polly')

Hello, Polly. Good morning!

Docstring

The docstring is short for documentation string and we use this to give a short description of what the function will do. This is optional but it is good practice to include it. In the example shown above, our docstring was straight after the header, and we would normally use triple quotes to allow the docstring to go over multiple lines.

For example:

>>> print(greet.__doc__)

This function will greet

the person passed into the

name parameter

The Return Statement

Return statements are used to exit the function and return to where the function was called. The syntax of the return function is:

return [expression_list]

The return statement may have an expression that will be evaluated and the value returned. If the statement does not have an expression or there is no return statement in the function, the return will be an object called None.

For example:

>>> print(greet("Mary"))

Hello, Mary. Good morning!

None

Here, the returned value is None.

This is an example of a return statement:

def absolute_value(num):

"""This function will return the absolute value of the number entered"""

if num >= 0:

return num

else:

return -num

 # Output: 2

print(absolute_value(2))

 # Output: 4

print(absolute_value(-4))

Scope and Lifetime of Variables

The variable's scope is the part of the program where the variable gets recognition. Any variable and parameters defined in a function cannot be seen from outside that function, and, as such, they are given local scope. The variable's lifetime is how long the variable is in memory before it exits. Inside a function, a variable will have a lifetime that lasts while the function continues to execute. Once the function has been returned, the variable is destroyed, and that is why functions never remember values from previously called variables.

The following example shows variable scope in a function:

def my_func():

x = 10

print("Value inside function:",x)

x = 20

my_func()

print("Value outside function:",x)

The output of this would be:

Value inside function: 10

Value outside function: 20

In this example, we can see that x is given an initial value of 20. Even though the value was changed to 10 by the my_func function, the value outside the function did not change. The reason is that the variable called x in the function is local to that function and has nothing to do with the one outside. Even though they have identical names, they are different variables and have different scopes.

That said, any variable outside the function can be seen from inside the function, and they are of global scope. These variables can be read from the function but cannot be changed. If we wanted to modify a variable's value from outside, they would need to be declared as a global variable, and this is done by using the reserved keyword, global, as part of the name.

Variable Function Arguments

Python allows us to define functions that can have several arguments, and there are 3 forms of this:

- Python Default Argument A function argument may be given a default value and we do this through = (the assignment operator), as shown below:

def greet(name, msg = "Good morning!"):

"""

This function will greet the person with the message we provided.

If the message is not given, it will default to "Good morning!"

"""

print("Hello",name + ', ' + msg)

greet("Kathy")

greet("Brian","How are you doing?")

The parameter name in this function doesn't have any default value and is mandatory in a function call. However, the msg parameter has a default value, which is "Good morning!" and this is optional in a function call. If we provide a value, the default value will be overwritten.

You can assign default values to any function arguments, but you must remember that, once you have got that default value, every argument to the right of the argument must also contain default values. I mean that you cannot follow a default argument with arguments that aren't default. For example, let's define the function header from the last example differently:

def greet(msg = "Good morning!", name):

You would see this error message:

SyntaxError: non-default argument follows default argument

Python Keyword Arguments

When functions are called, the values of the arguments are dependent on the argument position. In Python, we can call a function using keyword arguments, and the argument order may be altered. The next example shows several calls to the greet function; each will produce the same result and each is a valid way of doing this: >>> # 2 keyword arguments.

> *>>> greet(name = "Brian",msg = "How are you doing?")*

> *>>> # 2 keyword arguments (out of order)*

> *>>> greet(msg = "How are you doing?",name = "Brian")*

> *>>> # 1 positional, 1 keyword argument*

> *>>> greet("Brian",msg = "How are you doing?")*

As demonstrated, positional and keyword arguments can be mixed in a function call, so long as the keyword arguments come after the positionals. If you do it the other way, errors will be displayed:

> *greet(name="Brian","How are you doing?")*

This will result in this error:

> *SyntaxError: non-keyword arg after keyword arg*

Using Args and *Kwargs for Packing and Unpacking

*args

Args and *kwargs are generally used when defining a function; they let you pass variable arguments to one function. In this case, the variable indicates that you do not know how many arguments are to be passed by the user beforehand, so you use these keywords. *args sends an argument of variable length and with no keywords to the function. Here's an example: def test_var_args(f_arg, *argv):

> *print "first normal arg:", f_arg*
>
> *for arg in argv:*
>
> *print "another arg through *argv :", arg*
>
> *test_var_args(martha,snake,bacon,'test')*

This produces the following result:

> *first normal arg: martha*
>
> *another arg through *argv : snake*
>
> *another arg through *argv : bacon*
>
> *another arg through *argv : test*

**kwargs

kwargs are used to pass arguments of variable lengths with keywords to the function. **kwargs should be used if you are looking to handle any named arguments in your def greet_me(kwargs):

> *if kwargs is not None:*
>
> *for key, value in kwargs.iteritems():*
>
> *print "%s == %s" %(key,value)*
>
> *>>> greet_me(name="martha")*
>
> *name == martha*

This just shows you the basics of how args and *kwargs work and, if you haven't worked it out by now, args is short for arguments, and *kwargs is for keyword arguments. Next, we will look at using these to call functions with dictionaries or lists of arguments. Look at the following example: def test_args_kwargs(arg1, arg2, arg3):

print "arg1:", arg1

print "arg2:", arg2

print "arg3:", arg3

**args or **kwargs can be used to pass arguments to the function and here is how we do it:

 # first with *args

>>> args = ("two", 3,5)

>>> test_args_kwargs(*args)

arg1: two

arg2: 3

arg3: 5

 # now with **kwargs:

>>> kwargs = {"arg3": 3, "arg2": "two","arg1":5}

>>> test_args_kwargs(**kwargs)

arg1: 5

arg2: two

arg3: 3

If you want to use all 3 functions—args, *kwargs, and formal args then you would do it in this order:

some_func(fargs,*args,**kwargs)

Return Statement

Return statements are useful when you create functions whose sole job is to return some values. These could be for users or programmers alike. It is much easier if we do this instead of talking about theories, so let's jump back to our PyCharm and create another function.

Let us define a function called 'cube', which will multiply the number by itself 3 times. However, since we want Python to return a value, we will use the following code:

```
def cube(number):

return number number number
```

By typing 'return' you are informing Python that you wish to return a value to you that can later be stored in a variable or used elsewhere. It is pretty much like the input() function where a user enters something and returns it to us.

```
def cube(number):

return number number number

number = int(input("Enter the number: "))

print(cube(number))
```

Go ahead and try out the code to see how it works. You don't need to define functions such as these. You can create your complex functions, which convert kilos into pounds, miles into kilometers, or even carry out far greater and more complex jobs. The only limit is your imagination. The more you practice, the more you explore.

With that said, it is time to say goodbye to the world of functions and head into the advanced territories of Python. By now, you already have all you need to know to start writing your codes.

How to Define and Call Function?

To start, we need to look at how we can define our functions in this language. The function in Python will be defined when we use the statement of "def" and then follow it with a function name and some parentheses in place as well. This lets the compiler know that you are defining a function and which function you would like to define at this time. There will be a few rules in place when it comes to defining one of these functions, though, and it is important to do these properly to ensure your code acts in the way you would like. Some of the Python rules that we need to follow for defining these functions will include:

1. Any of the arguments or input parameters you would use have to be placed within the parentheses so that the compiler knows what is going on.

2. The function first statement can be optional—something like a documentation string that goes with your function if needed.

3. The code found within all of the functions that we are working with needs to start out with a colon, and then we need to indent it.

4. The statement return that we get, or the expression, will need to exit a function at this time. We can then have the option of passing back a value to the caller. A return statement that doesn't have an argument with it will give us the same return as None.

Before we get too familiar with some of the work that can be done with these Python functions, we need to take some time to understand the rules of indentation when we are declaring these functions in Python. The same kinds of rules will apply to some of the other elements of Python, such as declaring conditions, variables, and loops, so learning how this work can be important here.

You will find that Python is going to follow a particular style when it comes to indentation. This helps define the code because the functions in this language won't have any explicit beginning or end, like the curly braces in other languages to help indicate the start and the stop for that function. This is why we are going to rely on the indentation instead. When we work with the proper kind of indentation here, we can see some good results and ensure that the compiler knows when the function is being used.

Parameters

Parameters Require Arguments

You cannot call a function with parameters without an argument. If you do, you will receive an error. For example:

>>> *def sampFunc(x):*

print(x)

>>> *sampFunc()*

Traceback (most recent call last):

File "<stdin>", line 1, in <module>

TypeError: y() missing 1 required positional argument: 'x'

>>> _

Multiple Parameters

You can assign 2 or more parameters in a function. For example:

>>> *def simpOp(x, y):*

z = x + y

print(z)

>>> *simpOp(1, 2)*

3

>>> _

Return Statement

The return keyword makes a function return a value. For a simpler explanation, it makes the function be used as a variable that has an assigned or processed value. For example:

>>> *def concat(string1, string2):*

return string1 + string2

>>> *x = concat("Text1", "Text2")*

>>> *x*

'Text1Text2'

>>> *_*

A function can return a value even if it does not have parameters. For example:

>>> *def piString():*

return "3.14159265359"

>>> *x = piString()*

>>> *x*

'3.14159265359'

>>> *_*

As you can see, using the keyword method makes it simpler for you to retrieve a value from a function without relying on global variables. Return allows you to make clean and efficient code.

Chapter 6: Strings Method

Strings consist of more than one character. A string can be a constant or a variable. A string data type is the main unit of programming.

Create and Print Strings

Strings are surrounded by either 'or ". For that reason, to define a string, you need to enclose it with single or double-quotes.

For example:

"The first program."

'Second program.'

Its for you to you to decide if you want to use single or double-quotes. The one thing you need to ensure is that you become consistent.

String Concatenation

String concatenation is joining strings to create a new string. The + operator are useful when you want to perform string concatenation. Don't forget that if you use numbers, the + operator becomes an addition operator.

Example of how to concatenate strings:

Print ("Come" + "Back to school")

Still, you can place whitespace between strings.

When it comes to string concatenation, avoid using the + operator with diverse data types. For example:

Print ("First program" + 34)

This will output an error message.

But if you want to create a string like "feel23", you can do so by enclosing the number 23 in quotes. This will make it a string instead of an integer. Changing numbers into strings for concatenation is important when working with zip codes.

If you combine more than one string, you get a new string to use in the whole program.

Replication of String

Situations occur that demand the use of Python to automate functions, and one way to do this is by repeating a string multiple times. You can accomplish this with the * operator.

The * operator does a different function if used with numbers.

When you use it with a single string and integer, the * becomes the string replication operator. It will repeat a single string different times you want via the integer you offer.

For instance: This code will print the name Python 7 times without typing 7 times:

Print ("Python" * 7)

Using string replication, you can repeat a different string times you want.

How to Store String Variables?

Variables refer to symbols that one can hold data in a program. Think of variables as empty boxes that you enter data or value. As said before, strings are data, and you can use them to take the space of variables. Declaring a string as a variable can simplify the process of using strings in the whole of Python programs.

To keep a string within a variable, you need to allocate a variable to a string. For example:

My_string = "My son likes Pizza."

My_string is a variable. Now you can proceed to print My_string, which stores the data in string format.

Print(My_string)

This will output the result: My son likes Pizza.

Using variables in place of strings eliminates the need to retype a string every time you want to use it. This simplifies the process of coding and makes it easy to manipulate strings inside a program.

Uppercase and Lowercase Strings

In the strings functions, there is the function str.upper () and str.lower (), which outputs a string with all letters converted either to upper-case or lower-case letters. Since strings are "immutable," these functions create a new string.

Let us change the string "Wake up" to become upper case:

my_string = "wake up"

Print(my_string.upper())

Output

WAKE UP

Next, let us change the string to lower case:

Print(my_string.lower())

Output

wake up

The two string functions: str.upper() and str.lower() functions simplify the process of evaluation and string comparison by making the case consistent. That way, when a user writes their name in small letters, it is still possible to tell whether the name is in the database by looking at all-upper-case names.

Chapter 7: Conditional Statements and Loops

Another fun thing to work with in the Python language is the conditional statements. These are going to be known by many different names, such as the if statements and the decision control statements. But they will be a great option when you would like the program to learn how to do a few things on its own, without you having to think about all of the possible inputs before you even start.

There are going to be times when you would like to make sure that your code behaves in the right manner and can make some decisions on its own when you cannot be there to monitor it all and hope that it all fits into the right place. Any time that you have a part of your code that will allow the user to put in any kind of answer that they want all on their own, rather than just selecting from a few options, then you are going to find that the conditional statements are the best ones to work with.

Decision Making in Python

Decision-making statements will execute code only if a particular condition holds true. For instance, consider a student database containing student records with their aggregate marks. If we wanted to allocate a scholarship to a student with marks above 90%, a decision statement is used to determine if the marks are above 90% and then export that name.

The simplest form of a decision-making statement is the 'if' statement. The basic structure of this is shown below.

If (condition) : //Execute code

In the above abstract code snippet, we can see that the code will be executed based on the outcome of the 'if' condition. Only when the condition is true will the subsequent statements be executed. There are different types of decision-making statements, and in this chapter, we will go through each of them in more detail.

If Statement

The 'if' statement allows us to perform an action only if a certain condition evaluates to true. The general syntax of the 'if' statement is given below.

If (condition) : //Execute code

Let's now look at an example of how this loop can be used.

Example: The following program showcases the if statement.

 # Decision-making statements

a= 10

if (a == 10) : print("The value of a is 10")

This program's output will be as follows:

The value of a is 10

In the above program:

· We are first defining a variable called 'a'.

· The variable holds a value of 10.

Now we use the 'if' statement with the condition that checks whether 'a' is equal to 10.

If 'a' is indeed equal to 10, we print the statement to the console 'The value of a is 10'.

If-Else Statement

The 'if-else' statement is similar to the 'if' statement; however, it provides an additional option to execute another statement when the condition does not evaluate as true. The general syntax of the 'if-else' statement is given below.

if (condition) :

//Execute code

else:

//Execute code

Herewith the help of the 'else' clause, we can specify a code block, which can be executed if the condition evaluates to false. Let's look at an example of how this loop can be used.

Example: The following program shows how to use the if-else statement.

 # Decision making statements

a= 11

if (a == 10) : print("The value of a is 10")

else : print("The value of a is not equal to 10")

This program's output will be as follows:

Value of a is not equal to 10

In the above program:

· We are first defining a variable called 'a'.

· The variable holds a value of 11.

Now we use the 'if' statement, which has a condition that checks if the value of 'a' is equal to 10. If it is, a statement will be printed on the console.

We are also specifying an 'else' condition, which will print a different statement to the console if the value of 'a' does not equal 10.

In this example, the 'else' condition will be executed.

Pass Statement in Python

Like a comment, a pass statement does not impact the program, leading to no operation.

Think of a program code that you plan to use in the future but is not currently needed.

Instead of inserting that code in the future, the code can be written as pass statements.

Here's an example:

1. Start IDLE.

2. Navigate the File menu and click New Window.

3. Type the following:

my_list={'k','i','n'}

for tracker in my_list:

pass

The Python Loops

The next topic that we will need to take some time to discuss in this coding language is an idea that is known as a loop. These will be important to the codes you want to write, and they can work well when you combine them with a few of the conditional statements that we talked about before. Loops are a good way to clean up your program, they can ensure that you will see a lot of work done with just a few lines of code, and it is really a great way for us to make the code intense and powerful, without having to rewrite a bunch of things or learn a lot of complicated processes.

You will find that these loops will be helpful when you are writing out any of the codes you want that should repeat many times. This repeating needs to happen at least a few times in your code, but you want to do this without making the code messy and without having to go through and write out those lines a bunch of times, either.

For example, maybe you are going through and working on your code where you want to list out the numbers from one to 50. You don't really want to spend all of your time writing that many lines of code so that the compiler can learn what it should do. When you add in a loop, you will find that it can do some of your work. These loops basically tell the compiler to repeat itself until you set up a condition that tells it to stop.

You have 2 options to write out something like the one above. You can go through and type in all parts one at a time. Or you can go through and use a loop and get it done in just a few lines of code. We will look at the nested loop in a few pages and show you exactly how we can work with these loops for our needs.

While this process can sometimes sound a bit complex, you will find that these loops can be pretty easy to work with. These loops tell your compiler that it needs to repeat the same code block more than once. The compiler will continue reading through the same code block again until the inserted condition is met and ready to be used. So, if you want to allow the code to count from one to 50, you would just tell the compiler to read through the same lines of code until the output is higher than 50. We will take a look at a few of the codes that you will write out that can handle this problem for us. Of course, when writing a loop condition, you need to be careful about getting the condition set up. If you don't set up your condition from the beginning, then the program will just keep reading the code over and over again, getting stuck in a continuous loop. You need to have a condition or a break in your code to help it stop and move on to the next thing the program should do.

With the traditional methods of coding that you may have used in the past, you would have to write out every line of code. Even if some similar parts of code were the same, or you were basically retyping the same piece of code repeatedly, that is how you had to do it as a beginner because that is the only way that you knew how to do things.

With the help of these loops, you can get rid of that way of thinking. You can combine many lines of code into just a few and instead convince the compiler to read through that same line as many times as you need. If you need it to do it 100 times, then that is what the compiler will do. With one line of code, thanks to these loops, you can get a ton of things done without having to write out 100 lines, or more, of code.

With all of this said, there are a few options that you can choose when it is time to try out the loops. The method you will pick will depend on what you would like to happen in the program and how often you are hoping that the compiler will go through the loop at a minimum. We now look at the 3 most popular loops that show up in programming, including the nested loop, the while loop, and the for a loop.

The While Loop

On our list, we will start with the while loop. This while loop will be the type of loop that we will use if we would like to make sure our code will go through the cycle at least a minimum number of times. You can set how many times you would like the loop to happen when you are writing out the code to make sure that the loop will go through the process for as long as you need it.

With this kind of loop in Python, your goal will not be to have the code go through a cycle an indefinite number of times, but you do want to make sure that it can do it a specific number of times, the amount that will ensure your code works how you would like. Going back to our earlier example, if you want to have the program count from one to 50, you want to make sure that this program will head through the loop 50 times to finish it all off. With this option, the loop will go through the process a minimum of one time and then will check out whether the conditions of that loop have been met or not. It will put up the number one, then check to see whether this output meets the conditions, see that it does not, put in the number 2, and continue this loop until it sees that it is at a number higher than 50.

This is a simple kind of loop that we can work with and we are going to see how we can put it to practical use for some of the work that we want to do. To get a better idea of how we can get these loops to work, let's take a look at some of the sample codes of a while loop and see what is going to happen when it gets to work:

```
counter = 1

while(counter <= 3):

principal = int(input("Enter the principal amount:"))

numberofyears = int(input("Enter the number of years:"))

rateofinterest = float(input("Enter the rate of interest:"))

simpleinterest = principal numberofyears rateofinterest/100

print("Simple interest = %.2f" %simpleinterest)

#increase the counter by 1

counter = counter + 1

print("You have calculated simple interest for 3 time!")
```

Before we move on, take this code and add it to your compiler and let it execute this code. You will see that when this is done, the output will come out so that the user can place any information they want into the program. Then the program will do its computations and figure out the interest rates and the final amounts, based on whatever numbers the user placed into the system. With this particular example, we set the loop up to go through 3 times. This allows the user to put in results 3 times to the system before moving on. You can always change this around and add in more of the loops if it works the best for your program.

Working With the for Loop

Now we look at the while loop and see the benefits of working with that kind of loop. It is time for us to move on to the third type of loop we can use in this kind of coding. We will need to work with a slightly different idea in some of the coding that we want to do, and this is where we will want to bring in the for loop. Often, the work you will do with the while loop can also be done with the loop, and this loop is seen as the traditional form of working on loops, so you are more likely to see this one a lot in the coding you do.

With the for loop that we will work with, you will find that you can set all of this up so that the user will not be the one who goes through and provides the information to the loop on when it should stop. Instead, the loop will be set up to go over the iteration in the order that things will show up in the statement that you write, and then this information is the kind that will show up on the screen. With this, you will note that there isn't need for input from any outside force or even from the user, at least until your loop is done and reaches the end.

A good example of working with the for loop is going to include:

 # Measure some strings:

words = ['apple', 'mango', 'banana', 'orange']

for w in words:

print(w, len(w))

When you work with the above loop example, you can add it to your compiler and see what happens when it gets executed. When you do this, the 4 fruits that come out on your screen will show up in the exact order you have them written out. If you want to have them show up in a different order, you can do that, but you need to go back to your code and rewrite them in the right order or your chosen order. Once you have then written out in the syntax and are ready to be executed in the code, you can't make any changes to them.

The Nested Loop

And finally, we are going to take a look at the final type of loop, the one that is known as the nested loop. This one will work in a slightly different manner than we may see with the for loop and the while loop, but there are times when it can come in handy and will help us get a lot of things done in our coding. When we decide to work with one of the nested loops, you take one loop and then place it to go inside another loop. Then it is set up that both of these loops will continue to run until everything is done. This may seem silly to add to some of the codings that we do, and it may seem overly complicated for what we want to accomplish. But there are a lot of times when we will need this to show up in our codes. For example, maybe we want to create a code that can write out a multiplication table for us. Maybe you want to have it set up to multiply from one time one to 10 times 10.

If you went through and wrote this out by hand, which you certainly can if you would like, this would take an enormous amount of code to get it done and ensure the program will behave how you want. This is a lot of time and wasted energy, though, since you can easily just work with the nested loop to get it all done. This can get the work done in just a few lines of code, rather than hundreds of lines of code, and can save time. The code that you can use to create a nested loop and make your multiplication table will include:

#write a multiplication table from 1 to 10

For x in xrange(1, 11):

For y in xrange(1, 11):

*Print '%d = %d' % (x, y, x*x)*

When you got the output of this program, it is going to look similar to this:

1*1 = 1

1*2 = 2

1*3 = 3

1*4 = 4

All the way up to 1*10 = 2

Then it would move on to do the table by twos such as this:

2*1 =2

2*2 = 4

And so on until you end up with 10*10 = 100 as your final spot in the sequence.

Go ahead and put this into the compiler and see what happens. You will simply have 4 lines of code and end up with a whole multiplication table that shows up on your program. Think of how many lines of code you would have to write out to get this table the traditional way you did before? This table only took a few lines to accomplish, which shows how powerful and great the nested loop can be.

Boolean Methods

Python consist of string methods used to determine Boolean value. These methods are important when you want to create forms for users to complete. If we are requesting a postcode, you will only want to accept a numeric string.

It is important to verify whether characters are upper case, title case, or lower case because it improves the process of sorting data. Additionally, it creates room to standardize data collected by gathering and changing strings.

The Boolean string functions are important when you want to check if something that a user types suit a specific parameter.

Computing the Length Of A String

len () function it will count the number of characters in a string. This method is critical if you want to apply minimum or maximum password lengths. For instance, to truncate larger strings to fit specific limits for application in abbreviations.

To illustrate this method, you will determine the length of a sentence-long string:

```
open_source = "Sammy contributes to open source."
print(len(open_source))

Output
33
```

In this example, the variable open_source is set to equal the string, and then the variable is passed to len() method using len(open_source). The method is then passed to print () to determine the output on the screen from the program.

Remember that character is enclosed with single or double marks, including whitespace characters and symbols. These will be counted using the len() function.

Other ways you can use to change strings in Python is by using str.split(), str.join(), and str.replace () functions.

The str.join() function joins two strings but in a method in which it passes one string to another.

Whitespace

These are characters which the computer knows but readers cannot see. The most common type of whitespace is newlines, spaces, and tabs.

It is easy to create space because you have been using it since the time you have used computers. Newlines and tabs represent unique character combinations.

You can use tabs anyplace you want in a string.

The character combination for tabs is "\t" while a new line is represented by "\n."

Stripping a White Space

In most instances, you will let users type text into a box and then read the text and use it. It is simple for people to apply extra whitespace at the start or end of their text. Whitespace comprises newlines, tabs, and spaces.

In general, it is good to remove this whitespace from strings before you begin to work with them.

String Literals

Including string values in Python code is an easy thing. It will start and ends with a single quote. But the question is, how can you apply a quote inside a string? If you type "That is Mark's car." It will not work because Python considers the end of the string as Mark, and the remaining section is invalid. Luckily, there are many ways to enter strings.

Double Quotes

Strings can start and end with double quotes, just like it happens with single quotes. However, the advantage of double quotes is that the string can include a single quote character within it. In Python interactive shell, Type the following code:

```
>>> spam = "That is Mark's cat."
```

Since a string starts with a double quote, Python is aware that the single quote belongs to the string and doesn't end the string. But if you want to apply both single and double quotes in a string, you will have to apply escape characters.

Escape Characters

An escape character will allow you to include characters that are hard to insert a string. An escape character is made up of a backslash and the character you would like to include in the string. Although it has two characters, it is still called a singular escape character. For instance, the escape character for a single quote is \'. You can include this character into a string that starts and ends with a single quote. To learn how escape characters operate, type this code into the Python shell:

>>> spam = 'Say hello to Bob\'s mother.'

Python can tell from the backlash in a single quote in Bob\'s; this single quote is not the end of the string value. The escape characters \' and \" allow you to include single quotes and double quotes within your strings.

Raw Strings

You can include r before the start of the quotation mark of a string to create a raw string. A raw string will eliminate all escape characters and print backlash that occurs in the string. For example:

>>> print(r'That is Joyce\'s car.')

That is Joyce\'s car.

Since this is a raw string, Python treats the backslash as a member of the string and not at the beginning of an escape character. Raw strings are useful if you type string values that have numerous backslashes like the strings applied for regular expressions.

Multiline Strings

Although you can apply the \n escape character to insert a new line into a string, it is straightforward to apply multiline strings. A multiline string in Python starts and ends with three single quotes, or sometimes three double quotes. Any tabs, quotes, or newlines located between the "triple quotes" can be said to members of the string. The rules for Python indentation blocks do not work inside a multiline string.

Type the following in your file editor:

```
print('''Dear Alice,

Eve's cat has been arrested for catnapping, cat burglary, and extortion.

Sincerely,
Bob''')
```

You will have the following result If you run this code:

```
Dear Alice,

Eve's cat has been arrested for catnapping, cat burglary, and extortion.

Sincerely,
Bob
```

Keep in mind that a single quote character in Eve's doesn't have to be escaped. It is optional to escape single and double quotes in a raw string. A print () call would show identical text, but it doesn't apply a multiline string.

Multiline Comments

Even if the hash character indicates the start of a comment for the remaining line, a multiline string is always used for comments that extend multiple lines. Below is a genuine Python code:

```python
"""This is a test Python program.
Written by Al Sweigart al@inventwithpython.com

This program was designed for Python 3, not Python 2.
"""

def spam():
    """This is a multiline comment to help
    explain what the spam() function does."""
    print('Hello!')
```

Stripping Strings And Indexes

Consider a string like 'Hello world!' as a list, and every character inside the string is an item with an equivalent index.

```
' H  e  l  l  o     w  o  r  l  d   !  '
  0  1  2  3  4  5  6  7  8  9  10  11
```

In this example, space and exclamation marks are also counted. This gives you a total of 12.

Enter the following code:

```python
>>> spam = 'Hello world!'
>>> spam[0]
'H'
>>> spam[4]
'o'
>>> spam[-1]
'!'
>>> spam[0:5]
'Hello'
>>> spam[:5]
'Hello'
>>> spam[6:]
'world!'
```

Directly addressing an index gives you a character stored in that point. If you apply a range, the starting index must be counted, too.

Something else that you must remember is that slicing a string doesn't change the beginning of the string.

You can retain a slice from a certain variable in a separate variable. Try to enter the following into the interactive shell:

```
>>> spam = 'Hello world!'
>>> fizz = spam[0:5]
>>> fizz
'Hello'
```

Looping and Counting

When counting and looping, it is important to keep track of your original count by storing it with the code itself at all times. Counting is not as simple as 1, 2, 3, 4. You must first be able to initialize the counter with a starting value and then increment that value until it is greater than or equal to the length of your list. Once you have reached the end of the list with your looping operation, you must decrement your count by one.

Here is an example of some code that utilizes count and looping. The code below reads in a list of numbers and then prints these numbers on the screen. Before reading in the user's list, you must define what happens when there are no more numbers to read. Typically this would be –1, but using the modulus operator is just one way to accomplish this task. You can also use if, elif , or else statements inside of your loops to allow for different logic when determining how many times you should execute your loop.

The most important concept with counting is to use the same variable which is being incremented over and over again throughout your program. By doing this, you will avoid errors and be able to keep track of your count.

LOOP: Count numbers from 1 to 400: # Counting and looping for number in range(1,401): # Loop begins print("Inside loop") # Prints "Inside loop" print("The loop iterated %d times." % (number)) # Prints "The loop iterated 399 times" print("Outside loop")

Chapter 8: Lists

Lists are collections of data. When you think about a list in regular life, you often think of a grocery list or a to-do list. These lists are collections of items, and that's what precisely lists in Python are: collections of items. Lists are convenient because they offer quick and easy storage and retrieval of items.

We have several values that we need to access in our program. We could declare separate variables for all those values or store them all in a single variable as a list. Declaring a list is as simple as using brackets and separating objects in the list with commas. So, if we wanted to declare a list of fruits, we could do that by doing the following:

Fruits = ["apple", "pear", "orange", "banana"]

It's also possible to declare an empty list using empty brackets. You can later add items to the list with a specific function, the append function - append(). We can access the items in the list individually by specifying the position of the item that we want. Remember, Python is zero-based, so the first item in the list has a position of 0. How do we utilize the values from a list? We just declare a variable that references that specific value and position, as shown below:

Apple = fruits[0]

If you want to start by selecting items from the end of the list first, instead of the front, you can do this by using negative numbers. Passing "-1" into the brackets will give us the last item in the list while passing "-2" will select the second to last item. As you saw above, you can choose one item from a list and store it as a variable, but you can also choose multiple items from a list. This is achieved using the colon inside the brackets. The value on the left of the colon indicates the first value you'd like to select and the value on the right side of the colon, indicating where to stop selecting values. This means that if you had a list containing 6 items, the notation list. Would select the second item in the list (remember, zero-based) through the fourth item.

Using brackets and colons to select portions of a list is known as list slicing. When slicing a list, the slicing notation takes the item you want to get first as the first input and the item you want to end your search at as the second input. In order words, the item at the first index is included, but the item at the second index isn't. Going back to our list of fruits, if we sliced that list like so [0:2], we would only get "apple" and "pear" included in the slice because the second input specifies where we stop searching, which is the third value on the list.

You can also slice with the assistance of a third input, referred to as a stepper. If you had a list of numbers running from 0 to 8, you could slice it by getting every other number instead of every number from a starting point to an endpoint. Let's assume we want to slice the list of numbers and get every other number. We could do this by using the following commands:

numbers = [0, 1, 2, 3, 4, 5, 6, 7, 8]

numbers[0:9:2]

This notation instructs the interpreter to start at 0 and run until 9, getting every second number. The return value is a list, as shown below:

[0, 2, 4, 6, 8]

When slicing, default values will be used if you don't specify an input. For instance, the default value for the first input is the beginning of the list, while on the opposite end, the default value for the second input is the end of the list. This means that a slice like [:12] would start from the first item and run until the eleventh item on the list. In other words, [:12] is a shorthand version of writing [0:12].

Lists can be modified in several different ways. Items can be added or removed from the list, but the value of individual items in the list can be altered. To change the value of an item in a list, you declare which index of the list you want to alter, followed by the value you want to replace it with. For example, you could update the fourth item on a list to a value of 15 by doing the following:

Numbers[3] = 15

Adding items to a list can be accomplished with the append() function. The value you want to append to the list goes inside the parentheses. Call the function with a period and the function name after the list to which you want to append the item. In other words:

list_to_update.append(value)

Append function adds the item to the end of the list. With the remove function, you can delete an item from the list. Just specify the item's index that you want to remove when using the function. You write del followed by the index of the item or items in the list you would like to remove. For instance, the following code would drop the values starting at index 2 and ending at index 4 from the list "A." Please note that the last index is not inclusive, meaning the index 4 will not be deleted in this example.

del A[2:4]

If you want to remove a specific value, you could use the remove() function. The remove() function will remove the first item from the list that matches the input value. Please note that if your list contains multiple entries of that value, remove() function will only remove one entry, not all entries of that value.

list_to_update.remove(value)

If you want to insert values at a specific position in a list, you can use the insert() function. The insert() function takes in 2 values: the index where you'd like to insert the value, and the second is the value you want to insert. Insertions are made immediately before the specified index, so the specified index and everything after it will have their indexes bumped up by one.

The following command would have the effect of inserting a 12 before the fourth item in list "A."

A.insert(3, 12)

There's one more thing we should cover about lists. As you continue to learn about data structures and algorithms, you'll hear about lists and a related structure called an "array." When used outside of a Python programming context (i.e., in a general data structures context), an "array" is just a list of indexed items. In this pure data structure sense, a "list" is an improved version of an array that has more functionality, like being resized or having links between items that point to the next item in the list.

Python has arrays as well, in addition to lists. In Python, arrays allow you to access and manipulate the items directly. If you wanted to divide every element in an array by 4, you could do this easily. In contrast, dividing a list by 4 will throw an error. In practice, arrays don't see much use outside of mathematical and data science programming. If you intend to get into these fields, you should investigate arrays further, but for our purposes, we won't spend time delving into them as we did with lists.

Chapter 9: Dictionary

A dictionary is a data type that holds key-value pairs. These key-value pairs are called items. You will sometimes hear dictionaries referred to as associative arrays, hashes, or hash tables.

Dictionaries are created using comma-separated items between curly braces. The item starts with a key, is then followed by a colon, and is concluded with a value. The format isdictionary_name = {key_1: value_1, key_N: value_N}. Create an empty dictionary use:dictionary_name = {}.

You can accessed an item in a dictionary by key. To do so, enclose the key in a bracket immediately following the dictionary name. The format isdictionary_name[key].

> contacts = {'Jason': '555-0123', 'Carl': '555-0987'}
>
> jasons_phone = contacts['Jason']
>
> carls_phone = contacts['Carl']
>
> print('Dial {} to call Jason.'.format(jasons_phone))
>
> print('Dial {} to call Carl.'.format(carls_phone))

Output:

> Dial 555-0123 to call Jason.
>
> Dial 555-0987 to call Carl.

Not only you can access values by key, you can also set values by key. The format isdictionary_name[key] = value.

> contacts = {'Jason': '555-0123', 'Carl': '555-0987'}
>
> contacts['Jason'] = '555-0000'
>
> jasons_phone = contacts['Jason']
>
> print('Dial {} to call Jason.'.format(jasons_phone))

Output:

> *Dial 555-0000 to call Jason.*

Adding Items to a Dictionary

adding new items to a dictionary through assignment. The format isdictionary_name[new_key] = value. determining the number of items in a dictionary use thelen() built-in function and pass in a dictionary.

> *contacts = {'Jason': '555-0123', 'Carl': '555-0987'}*
>
> *contacts['Tony'] = '555-0570'*
>
> *print(contacts)*
>
> *print(len(contacts))*

Output:

> *{'Jason': '555-0123', 'Carl': '555-0987', 'Tony': '555-0570'}*

Removing Items From a Dictionary

Use thedelstatement to remove an item from a dictionary. The format isdel dictionary_name[key].

> *contacts = {'Jason': '555-0123', 'Carl': '555-0987'}*
>
> *del contacts['Jason']*
>
> *print(contacts)*

Output:

> *{'Carl': '555-0987'}*

The values stored in a dictionary do not have to be of the same data type. In the following example, the value for theJasonkey is a list while the value for theCarl key is a string.

```
contacts = {

'Jason': ['555-0123', '555-0000'],

'Carl': '555-0987'

}

print('Jason:')

print(contacts['Jason'])

print('Carl:')

print(contacts['Carl'])
```

Output:

```
Jason:

['555-0123', '555-0000']

Carl:

555-0987
```

Additional spaces were used to improve readability when assigning the items to the contacts dictionary. Python will ignore the extra spaces as long as the syntax is followed.

Since the dictionary_name['key_name']stores its associated value, you can act upon it like the actual values themselves. For example, let's use a for loop for all Jason's phone numbers.

```
contacts = {

'Jason': ['555-0123', '555-0000'],

'Carl': '555-0987'

}
```

```python
for number in contacts['Jason']:

    print('Phone: {}'.format(number))
```

Output:

```
Phone: 555-0123

Phone: 555-0000
```

Chapter 10: Tuples

A tuple in Python is an ordered collection of objects. These also belong to the sequence data types like lists. Unlike lists, tuples are immutable, i.e., they cannot be changed after they are declared.

Creating a Tuple

Tuples can easily be created by putting elements inside parentheses/round brackets (()). The elements are separated from each other using the comma symbol. Indices in Tuples also start with 0, where the first element is placed at the 0th index.

We can create nested tuples by putting a tuple inside another tuple.

Creating a tuple that holds some alphabetical characters can be done as follows:

tuple_1 = ('a', 'b', 'c', 'y', 'z')

Note: If we have only a single element inside a tuple, we must place a comma value after the element to indicate the tuple.

tuple_2 = ('Ram',) is the correct way instead of tuple_2 = ('Ram'). The former with a comma after the element is interpreted as a tuple, whereas the latter is interpreted as a string by the interpreter. To understand this, take a look at the following code snippet:

```
tuple_1 = ('A', 'B', 'C', 'Y')
print(type(tuple_1))
print('Original tuple_1 is: ',tuple_1)
tuple_2 = ('Ram',)
print(type(tuple_2))
tuple_3 = ('Ram')
print(type(tuple_3))
```

Output

```
= RESTART: C:\Users\Saurabh Gupta\AppData\Local\Programs\Python\Python39\if.py =
<class 'tuple'>
Original tuple_1 is: ('A', 'B', 'C', 'Y')
<class 'tuple'>
<class 'str'>
>>>
```

We can see how variables tuple_2 and tuple_3 are interpreted differently by the interpreter.

Accessing Elements Inside a Tuple

As we did in the list, we can use both the positive and negative indices to access elements stored inside a tuple. The below is a code snippet showing how it can be done.

```
tuple_1 = ('A', 'B', 'C', 'Y')
print('Original tuple_1 is: ',tuple_1)
print('Printing the first element at 0th index: ',tuple_1[0])
print('Printing the second element at 1st index: ',tuple_1[1])
print('Printing the fourth element at 3rd index: ',tuple_1[3])
print('Printing the first element from last: ',tuple_1[-1])
print('Printing the third element from last: ',tuple_1[-3])
```

The output of the above-given source code will be given as:

```
= RESTART: C:\Users\Saurabh Gupta\AppData\Local\Programs\Python\Python39\if.py =
Original tuple_1 is: ('A', 'B', 'C', 'Y')
Printing the first element at 0th index:  A
Printing the second element at 1st index:  B
Printing the fourth element at 3rd index:  Y
Printing the first element from last:  Y
Printing the third element from last:  B
>>> |
```

Tuple Slicing

Tuple slicing can obtain a sequence of elements from the tuple. It can be done in the same manner that we used for lists. Take a look at the following example:

```
tuple_1 = ('A', 'B', 'C', 'Y',1,10,100,50,'Sum','Bob')
print('Original tuple_1 is: ',tuple_1)
print('Printing elements starting from 0th index to 3rd index: ',tuple_1[0:4])
print('Printing elements starting from 2nd index to 5th index: ',tuple_1[2:4])
print('Printing elements starting from 1st index to 6th index with step 2: ',tuple_1[1:7:2])
print('Printing elements starting from 0th index to the last index with step 3: ',tuple_1[::3])
```

Output

```
= RESTART: C:\Users\Saurabh Gupta\AppData\Local\Programs\Python\Python39\if.py =
Original tuple_1 is: ('A', 'B', 'C', 'Y', 1, 10, 100, 50, 'Sum', 'Bob')
Printing elements starting from 0th index to 3rd index:  ('A', 'B', 'C', 'Y')
Printing elements starting from 2nd index to 5th index:  ('C', 'Y', 1, 10)
Printing elements starting from 1st index to 6th index with step 2:  ('B', 'Y', 10)
Printing elements starting from 0th index to the last index with step 3:  ('A', 'Y', 100, 'Bob')
>>> |
```

Manipulating Elements Inside a Tuple

Updating the Values Inside a Tuple

As tuples are immutable, we cannot use the assignment operator to update values inside a tuple.

Suppose we have a tuple:

tuple_1 = ('A', 'B', 'C', 10, 100, 50)

And we want to update the element at index 1, i.e., the character 'B' with a character 'M', it cannot be done using the assignment operator as:

tuple_1 [1] = 'M'

(it is wrong; the interpreter will generate a TypeError in this case)

However, if the tuples consist of any mutable object inside them, they can be manipulated.

Also, we can use the '+' and '*' operators to perform concatenation and repetition of the elements present inside the tuple. Here's the following example:

```
tuple_1 = ('A', 'B', 'C')
tuple_2 = (10,100,50)

print('Original tuple_1 is: ',tuple_1)

print('Original tuple_2 is: ',tuple_2)

tuple_3 = tuple_1 + tuple_2

print('resultant tuple after concatenation is', tuple_3)

tuple_4 = tuple_2 * 3

print('resultant tuple_2 after repetition is', tuple_4)
```

Output

```
= RESTART: C:\Users\Saurabh Gupta\AppData\Local\Programs\Python\Python39\if.py =
Original tuple_1 is: ('A', 'B', 'C')
Original tuple_2 is: (10, 100, 50)
resultant tuple after concatenation is ('A', 'B', 'C', 10, 100, 50)
resultant tuple_2 after repetition is (10, 100, 50, 10, 100, 50, 10, 100, 50)
>>>
```

Removing/Deleting Elements From a Tuple

Earlier, elements inside a tuple couldn't be updated, so we could not remove a particular element from a tuple. However, removing the entire tuple is possible. It could be done using the del keyword. Let's look at the following example:

```
tuple_1 = ('A', 'B', 'C')

print('Original tuple_1 is: ',tuple_1)

del tuple_1

print(tuple_1)
```

After we save and run this script, the output will be obtained as:

```
» RESTART: C:\Users\Saurabh Gupta\AppData\Local\Programs\Python\Python39\if.py »
Original tuple_1 is:  ('A', 'B', 'C')
Traceback (most recent call last):
  File "C:\Users\Saurabh Gupta\AppData\Local\Programs\Python\Python39\if.py", li
ne 7, in <module>
    print(tuple_1)
NameError: name 'tuple_1' is not defined
>>>
```

We can notice here after we use the del keyword to remove the entire tuple and then try to print it, the interpreter throws us a NameError saying it is not defined.

Built-In Tuple Functions and Methods

A few built-in functions are used with tuples to get certain outputs that are shown in the table below:

Function Name	Description
len(tuple)	It returns total number of elements present inside a tuple.
tuple(sequence)	It is a tuple constructor that takes lists as inputs and converts them into a tuple.
max(tuple)	It returns the maximum element inside a tuple.
min(tuple)	It returns the minimum element inside a tuple.
cmp(tuple 1, tuple 2)	These are used to compare 2 tuples.

Also, we can use the in and not in operator to take the membership test, as we read in the case of lists.

Advantages of Tuple Over List

The immutable property of tuples makes it advantageous over lists in a variety of ways that are listed below:

In terms of speed, it is faster to iterate through a tuple as compared to a list. This creates a slight boost in performance.

Tuples are generally used for storing heterogeneous data types, whereas lists are used for storing homogenous data types.

If we want our data to be write-protected (it can't be manipulated), we keep it inside tuples.

Chapter 11: Classes

Fundamentals of Classes

Object-oriented programming is a style that changed how software institutions work. Object-oriented programming provides several practical approaches to writing software when working with teams. Python as a programming language supports both functional and object-oriented programming styles. As a Python programmer, you must understand and distinguish between classes and objects to write a program representing real-world things and their instances.

What Are Classes and Objects?

Classes represent real-world things in a program code. They act as a blueprint so that programmers can easily interact with real-world things for different situations. This prototype creates objects, and these object characteristics are usually written whenever you make a class.

Classes help programmers to bundle various functionalities into a single entity. Every time you create an object from a class, it will have all the behaviors you provided when you made a class. In addition, programmers can give every object unique traits to interact more efficiently. Object-oriented programming has an incredible relatability with real-world application use cases, and hence it is currently the most popular programming paradigms in the industry.

Classes help programmers reduce the boilerplate code and define the same instances repeatedly. Besides making things simpler, object-oriented programming also allows programmers to write complex code with a simple instantiation and many instances.

How to Create and Use a Class

Python provides a simple syntax rule to create classes in Python.

Class ClassName :

Example:

Class Cat:

Here, "Cat" is the class name. Remember that you cannot use reserved keywords for class names. Let us now create a simple example about cats using Python classes.

Example:

Class Cat():

" This is used to model a Cat."

Def __init__(self, breed, age) :

""" Initialize breed and age attributes """

self.breed = breed

self.age = age

Def meow(self) :

""" This describes about a cat meowing """

print(self.breed.title() + " cats meow loudly")

Def purr(self)

""" This describes about a cat purring """

print(self.breed.title() + " cats purrs loudly")

Explanation

Firstly, we have created a class with the name Cat. There are no attributes or parameters in the parentheses of the class because this is a new class where we are starting everything from scratch. Advanced classes may have many parameters and attribute to solve complex problems required for real-world applications.

Immediately after the class name, a docstring called ' This is used to model a cat' describes the necessity for this class. It would be best to practice writing docstrings more often to help other programmers understand the details about your class.

In the next step, we created an _init_ () method and defined 3 arguments. Python runs this unique function automatically when an object instance is created from a class. _init_ function is a mandatory Python function; without it, the interpreter will reject the object initiation.

Similarly, we have created 2 other functions, ' meow' and ' purr', with arguments for each. In this example, these 2 functions just print a statement. In real-world scenarios, methods will perform higher-level functionalities.

You should have observed the ' self' argument in all the 3 methods in the above class. Self is an automatic function argument that needs to be entered for every method in a class.

In a class, all the variables can be called using a dot operator (.). For example, ' self.age' is an example for calling a variable using a dot operator.

Exercises:

· Write a Python program that will import all the essential classes in Pandas machine learning library.

· Use a built-in module in Python to list out all the built-in functions that Python supports. Create a Python program to list all these functions in a table format.

· Using object-oriented programming, create an OOP model for a library management system. Introduce all the modules that can be used and list all the arguments that need to be given.

· Write a Python class of shapes to calculate the area of any figure.

· Write a class and create both global and instance class variables.

· Use Python classes to convert Roman numerical standards to the decimal system.

What Are Class and Instance Variables?

When using objects to amplify your program features, you need to use 2 types of variables: instance and class variables.

Class Variables

Variables are first used to store information with a significant identifier. A class variable is specifically created to provide a programming component for a consistent time. Creating a class variable can be used anywhere in the program without worrying about unsupported or import errors. All these class variables are usually entered during class construction.

The problem with class variables is that programmers cannot initialize from an instance variable.

Syntax:

Class example

Game = " Football"

Here Game is a class variable with a value of "Football".

Class variables can be added and replaced easily, making it an easy option for dynamic Python programs and software programmers.

Instance Variables

Instance variables are variables that are created explicitly for this purpose. Programmers cannot provide them with variables that are different. Many instance variables are defined within the class itself, and hence it becomes difficult for beginners to understand how they can be replaced or how dynamic allocation can be provided. While there are many ways to create memory allocation for the programs, you cannot use instance variables for universal programs.

You can efficiently work with class and instance variables to create evergreen software.

What Are Class and Static Methods?

Functions are different types. They provide value and information to the reader. They can be used to do a simple thing again and again. Programmers can use both class methods and static methods according to Python. Python also provides details about built-in functions.

Class Method

A class method is a built-in method evaluated when every function is created. A class method is like a constructor for Python programs and can receive implicit first arguments to make instances repeat easily.

When you use a class method, you cannot find the object of the class. A class method is implicit and is also said to receive instant information otherwise not controlled and provided by any object in the class.

Class methods should be bound to various instance variables that are already present.

You should also use a class parameter that can provide multiple information about classes and instances that are present right now in the program cycle.

All the variables can be modified and called instances for the class.

Static Method

A static method is a specific programming analysis that Python founders provide to help Python programmers understand the importance of static arguments common in other high-level languages such as Swift and C.

Many objects present in the class are augmented and cannot be ignored by the present instance classes. Not everyone can use classes to decide what their modifying function should be.

To know the differences between static and instance classes, you need to know both static and instance method constructors. All these constructors have parameters that cannot change because they correlate with functions that are not easy to create.

Many do not try to understand the essence of Parameters as they are created to extract information from methods efficiently. Also, as a Python programmer, you should find different ways to make literals understand why it is essential to use code that can be changed and extracted using data such as class methods. As a programmer, you would also need to be aware of statically supported methods that can interact with standard modules of other Python software.

Rectangle

Solving an equation involves translating the equation into a set of instructions that solve that equation. $A = B / C$ is equivalent to "$x = y / z$".

A rectangle is defined by 4 straight lines, 2 of which are parallel and intersect at right angles. The line segments between the 2 parallel lines form the rectangle's edges or bounding box.

The bounding box can be found by finding the distance between any 2 points on edge, calculating their midpoint, then splitting each side length in half to find their average value (the perpendicular height of one side divided by its width), taking the square root of that number.

It is also possible to find the bounding box using the Pythagorean theorem. The distance between the midpoints of the sides on a rectangle is equal to half of their hypotenuse, l divided by d, where l is the length of a side and d is the width of a side. The sides of a rectangle can be found this way: start at any 2 sides and calculate their length from point to point. The perpendicular height from one point to another on those sides gives you one half-side. Calculate that side's length from point to point twice, then take the square root of that number. This gives you the rectangle's midpoint. The second side of the rectangle is one-half-side away from the first side, on that point's perpendicular height. This will give you the width of that side.

The Pythagorean theorem can also be used to find the area of a rectangle. The length squared plus width squared equals this value, equal to both the length times itself plus 2 times the width times itself (l2+w2=A).

Solving equations is translating the equation into a language of statements. In this case, the language is Python statements. For rectangles, 2 relationships apply: The distance between any 2 points on a side equals one-half of that side's width times the point-to-point distance from one point to another on that same side. The Pythagorean theorem can be used to find the area of a rectangle given its length and width.

Conclusion

Thank you for reading this book. The power of programming languages in our digital world cannot be underestimated. People are increasingly reliant on the modern conveniences of smart technology, and that momentum will endure for a long time. With all the instructions provided in this book, you are now ready to start developing your own innovative smart tech ideas and turn them into a major tech startup company and guide humanity towards a smarter future.

It is by no means a comprehensive lesson on coding, but I hope that I have been able to give you the basics enough for you to be able to move on and expand your learning.

The thing about computer programming is that your learning will never stop. Even if you think you have the basics down pat, you don't use what you have learned regularly. Computer programming is changing almost daily, and it's up to you to keep up with everything that is going on. To that end, you would be well advised to join a few of the Python communities. You will find many of these on the internet, and they are places where you can stay up to the minute with changes, where you can join in conversations, discuss code, and ask for help.

Eventually, you will be in a position of being able to help the newbies on the scene, and it is then that you will realize just how far you have come.

Don't just read it once and think that you know it all because you don't. Trying to take in pages and pages of code and information will not serve you well, and it isn't a case of being the quickest to read it. You can read as much as you like, but anything else will be meaningless once your brain stops taking the information in.

Take your time; do the exercises as many times as you need to until you can write the answers AND understand the answers in your sleep. That is important—it is not enough to know the answers with Python programming. You have to be able to understand WHY the answer is such. The process that gets to that answer is that if you don't understand the code from start to finish, you will never understand the answers.

Python is a valuable programming language with a large array of uses. It is practical, efficient, and extremely easy to use. It will be a great asset and reference point for your future in programming. If you can think of it, you can create it. Don't be afraid to try something new.

Remember that knowledge is useless without application. Learning how to program without actual programming will only waste the time you invested in this book.

This book is meant to help a beginner programmer learn Python. You should write basic programs and even more complex programs with multiple objects with this book.

We provided plenty of exercises for you to practice your programming. Becoming a Pythonista will require plenty of practice. Also, feel free to devise your exercises and practice. Good luck and happy programming!

www.ingramcontent.com/pod-product-compliance
Lightning Source LLC
LaVergne TN
LVHW082035050326
832904LV00005B/189